The Spruce from Queensbury

by Mary Jean DeSantis

Illustrated by Anthony Richichi

Published in 2024 by
Saratoga Springs Publishing, LLC
Saratoga Springs, NY 12866
www.SaratogaSpringsPublishing.com
Printed in the United States of America

ISBN-13: 978-1-955568-51-7
ISBN-10: 1-955568-51-0
Library of Congress Control Number:
On file with Publisher
Text and illustrations Copyright © 2024

Written by Mary Jean DeSantis
Illustrations by Anthony Richichi
Graphic Design by Aimee Davis
Book design by Vicki Addesso Dodd

Saratoga Springs Publishing's books are
available at a discount when purchased in quantity for
promotions, fundraising and educational use.
For additional information, book sales or events,
contact us at www.ADKyou.com or llm.desantis@gmail.com

Scan here to ORDER ADDITIONAL BOOKS or learn more about
The 91st Tree from Queensbury through images and videos.

In loving memory of Ange

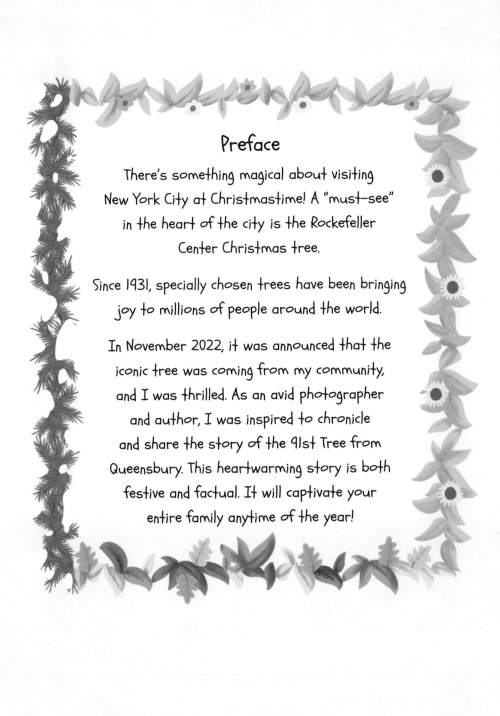

Preface

There's something magical about visiting New York City at Christmastime! A "must-see" in the heart of the city is the Rockefeller Center Christmas tree.

Since 1931, specially chosen trees have been bringing joy to millions of people around the world.

In November 2022, it was announced that the iconic tree was coming from my community, and I was thrilled. As an avid photographer and author, I was inspired to chronicle and share the story of the 91st Tree from Queensbury. This heartwarming story is both festive and factual. It will captivate your entire family anytime of the year!

It was a chilly November morning at Queensbury Elementary School. Miss Romano's students entered the classroom, ready for another fun-filled day.

"Good morning, everyone. Please hang up your coats and backpacks, and join me on the carpet. I have something very exciting to tell you!"

"I heard on the news last night that the Rockefeller Center Christmas Tree was chosen from Queensbury this year."

"What's the Rockefeller Center Christmas Tree?" asked Andy.

"It's a very special tree that's displayed in New York City during the holiday season, and it's chosen by a man named Mr. Erik," said Miss Romano.

"Who's Mr. Erik?" asked Debbie.

"He's a professional gardener at Rockefeller Center,
a very famous place in New York City."

"Many people call him *The Santa Claus of Christmas Trees!*"

"Where does Mr. Erik find the tree?"
asked Harrison.

"Well, the tree needs to be REALLY tall,
so he looks in forests all throughout
the Northeast. And people send him
pictures of their own trees, hoping
that theirs will be chosen."

"And that's just what happened this year. Mr. Erik received a photograph of a beautiful Norway spruce in Glens Falls, New York."

LOCATION: Glens Falls, NY

"So, in May, Mr. Erik took a road trip to see the tree."

"Wait, isn't that too early to pick out a Christmas tree?" asked Mike.

"Yes, for us it is, but not for Mr. Erik. He has to choose his tree several months before the holidays. It takes a long time and a lot of work to prepare such a big tree for the trip to New York City."

"While Mr. Erik was driving to Glens Falls, he noticed another beautiful tree in the neighboring town of Queensbury." *Wow, he thought, I'll have to go back and take a closer look.*

Later that afternoon,
Mr. Erik went back, walked
around the tree, and knew at
that moment he'd found the
next Rockefeller Center
Christmas Tree!

"IN QUEENSBURY!" shouted Maggie.

"YES, but he still needed to ask the owners if they'd
be willing to donate their tree."

So, he rang the doorbell, but no one was home. Mr. Erik
left his business card, and a few hours later,
he and the owner spoke on the phone.

The kind man agreed to give Mr. Erik his beautiful tree, saying,
"If it'll bring peace, hope, and joy to everyone who sees it,
then I'm happy to share it."

The next day, they met to discuss Mr. Erik's big plans for the tree.
They shook hands, and promised to keep its
location a secret until November, when an official
announcement would be made.

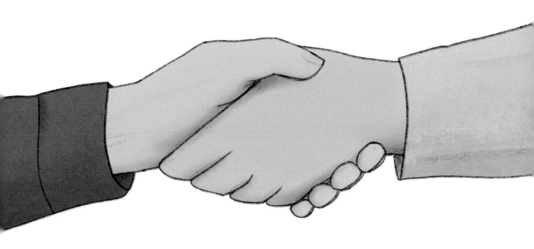

Mr. Erik had no time to waste! *The Santa Claus of Christmas Trees* got right to work caring for his new-found tree. Throughout that summer and fall, Mr. Erik took weekly trips to measure,

water, and feed the tree, without anyone in the community knowing.

It was his secret mission!

"OK kids, you've been sitting very nicely. Let's stand up and get moving! When I say go, jump up and down, and count by 10s until I say STOP."

"Ready, set, go!"

"Why did we stop at 90?" asked Douglas.

"Because for the past 90 years, a big, beautiful tree has been displayed in the heart of New York City at Christmastime."

"And we're SO lucky because a tree has never been chosen from OUR hometown, until THIS year!

Let's all cheer, the 91st Tree from Queensbury."

"Does that mean our town is famous?" asked Romi.

Miss Romano chuckled, "Queensbury isn't really famous, but this tree will always be part of our local history."

"How big is the tree?" Delaney asked.

"It's 82 feet high, so they have to use a powerful chainsaw
to cut through its huge trunk."

"Miss Romano, does *The Santa Claus of Christmas Trees* fly the tree to New York City in his sleigh?" asked Leo.

"No, unfortunately, he can't do that, it's much too big."

"Then how does it get there?" asked Kathleen.

"By a VERY LONG trailer, that's used to haul VERY BIG trees."

I really hope I can go see our tree in New York City", said Nova. Miss Romano replied, "So do I, that would be awesome! Well kids, I'd love to keep talking about the tree, but now it's time to line up for Art."

Throughout the school day, Delaney couldn't stop thinking about her hometown tree. She even drew a picture of it in Art class! When she got home, Delaney asked her mom if they could go see the tree.

"Absolutely! Hop in the car!"

The 91ˢᵗ TREE FROM QUEENSBURY

When they arrived, Delaney couldn't believe her eyes.
"Wow, it's HUGE," she shouted.

Mr. Erik's crew was hard at work in and around the tree.

"Mommy, is that *The Santa Claus of Christmas
Trees* over there?"

"Yes, I think so, Delaney."

As soon as Mr. Erik saw the little girl, he picked up a pinecone, walked over, and gently placed it in her hands.

"Oh, is this from the Christmas tree?" she asked.

Mr. Erik nodded yes. "Thank you so much, I'm gonna keep it forever!"

"What's your name?" he asked.

"I'm Delaney and this is my mom. My teacher told us all about the tree in school today, and I couldn't wait to see it! What are they doing with the rope?"

"My helpers are wrapping the branches, so they won't bend or break on the long trip to New York City."

A few days later, Delaney and her mom went back to see the tree, but the giant evergreen looked very different.

"What happened to the tree?" they asked. "Don't worry, my crew had to wrap it tightly, so it'll fit on the truck. I promise the tree will be beautiful again... just wait and see!"

After months of hard work, *The Santa Claus of Christmas Trees* and his merry "elves" geared up to cut down the massive Norway spruce.

91 ST TREE FROM QUEENSBURY!

WE ♥ QBY!

HOME TOWN

ROCKEFELLER CENTER

Hundreds of curious people were there to see the tree come down.

Delaney and her mom were there, too. The excited little girl was holding a sign that read, "Have a safe trip to NYC!!!" She caught the attention of the crowd, as well as TV news reporters.

Vroom, vroom, vroom. The spectators watched in silence as the chainsaw sliced through the tree's gigantic trunk, taking only four minutes to make a clean cut!

A huge crane held on tightly to the 28,000-pound tree.

It was slowly carried to the truck, carefully lowered, and wrapped with a colorful banner.

The tree was finally ready for its 200-mile journey to Rockefeller Plaza. Everyone breathed a huge sigh of relief! It was a job well done.

Souvenirs of freshly cut branches, pinecones, and seed packets were handed out to a few lucky spectators.

Throughout the day, Mr. Erik spoke with reporters, who were there to capture the big event. In one final interview, *The Santa Claus of Christmas Trees* said, "I'd like to thank the community for their support. This area is amazing, and it has great restaurants too!" With a chuckle, he patted his belly and said, "I really hope I can still fit into my Santa suit on Christmas Eve!"

When the engine on the big truck began to rumble, everyone pointed their cameras at Queensbury's soon-to-be-famous tree.

With a goodbye honk of his horn and a thumbs up to the crowd, the driver slowly pulled away, hauling his precious cargo. The 100-year-old evergreen was headed south for its new adventure.

Young and old cheered and waved as the tree was driven down Main Street, respectfully led by New York State Troopers.

It passed under a huge American flag...
an honorable send-off from a proud community.

After its two-day trip, a few hundred
people stood in the cold rain to
welcome Queensbury's tree
to Midtown Manhattan.

The next day, the family who donated the tree had the honor of hammering a spike into its trunk, following a yearly tradition. Then, the 14-ton Norway spruce was lifted into place.

Framework, called scaffolding, was built around the towering tree so it could be safely decorated with 50,000 multicolored lights and topped with a 900-pound crystal star!

During the tree-lighting ceremony,
the final countdown began...

5...4...3...2...1!

WOO-HOO!

The 91st tree was lit!
Let the holiday season begin!

On a cloudy December day, Delaney, her parents, and a bus full of excited people traveled from upstate New York to see the tree all "decked out" for the holidays.

The second she got off the bus and saw the tree, Delaney said, "It's so cool, like I can't believe my eyes, 'cause it's SO TALL!" This time, she held up a sign which read, "Glad you made it safe to NYC!"

After a long,
busy day in the Big Apple,
the proud family
returned to see the
festive tree one more
time. Its twinkling lights
and bright star looked
even more dazzling
at night.

Delaney gazed up and
shouted, "Thanks for
making everyone so
happy!", and she waved
goodbye.

The following week, Delaney was interviewed by local TV reporters. She happily chatted about her hand-made signs, her fun trip to New York City, and of course, her hometown tree, now being admired by millions of people all around the world!

In mid-January, the decorations were removed, and the Norway spruce was taken down, but the 91st tree still had one final purpose. Its trunk was cut into lumber and used to build homes for families in need.

As for *The Santa Claus of Christmas Trees*, he's
ALWAYS on the lookout for the next "perfect" tree.
And who knows? If you combine that tiny, little seed with the
"Magic" of Christmas, he might just find the next Rockefeller
Center Christmas Tree in your hometown...
you just have to BELIEVE!

About the Author

Mary Jean DeSantis, a retired speech & language pathologist, is the award-winning author of the children's book, "Where Are You, Alfie?" Mary owns an English Cream Golden Retriever, named Bryn, who is a certified therapy dog. Bryn is also the inspiration for Mary's next children's book. A few of Mary's favorite activities are pickle ball, hiking, and photography. A few of Bryn's favorite activities are hiking, playing with her doggie friends, and visiting with local senior citizens. Mary is delighted to share this heartwarming story of her community. She resides in Glens Falls, NY, aka "Hometown USA."

About the Illustrator

Anthony Richichi is an award-winning illustrator and painter from Upstate New York who has showcased his artwork in museums and national art publications throughout the world. *The 91st Tree From Queensbury* is one of over a dozen children's books Anthony has illustrated with Saratoga Springs Publishing, including his Colorworld series, which he also wrote. Anthony has also provided licensed artwork for the entertainment industry, including Marvel's *Spider Man*, the *Transformers*, and his award-winning band, Lock 9. Currently residing in his Adirondack art studio, he is lovingly surrounded by books, musical instruments, and lots of paintings.

Made in the USA
Columbia, SC
11 December 2024

47860660R00033